Rough Sea

Rough Sea

poems

J.P. White

GRAYSON BOOKS
West Hartford, Connecticut
graysonbooks.com

For Kat
who makes of every day, a promise

"There was a star riding through clouds one night,
& I said to the star, 'Consume me'."
—Virginia Woolf, *The Waves*

Contents

Canoe

And then, why not, climb back into the canoe,
set out into current, trusting your one good shoulder
that ten miles on the St. Croix is not too fierce
a number and the slight headwind nothing to worry
the old knots in you, because there with Kat,
I get one more day in September on the fringe
of change and there near the bank, four otters
recline a log to crack a stash of mussels.
I settle into their savoring without thinking
I should be elsewhere. Anything more to add?
This river light, where otters chirp and bob
and share the feast, must go on without us.
Like a brush of your fingers against my chin
when I ask you to come closer at night
and the bright river still there and waiting.

Dusk in March, 755, China, Civil War

What is it about the life of Tu Fu
that makes me feel like there's still hope for America?
He never finds a steady gig as a poet.
What few jobs he secures, he loses to the next tyrant.
He never collects anything like Medicare or Social Security.
His short run of 58 years is one of poverty, displacement,
menacing armies and perilous mountain crossings
combined with malaria, asthma, arthritis
which might all be other names
for homesickness. He is almost always leaving
and turning this moment into the next unshackling.
He seems to welcome his time alone and together
with the clear vanishing of everything.
Almost every chosen route includes a tenuous detour.
Fires and floods are not uncommon.
How can he bear it? All those fatal causes
demanding he alter course again and again
with no certainty a single loved one
will be alive once he arrives?
Hope from such a shambling between heaven and earth?
Like he is still there at dusk and here with us:
A poet on the road stopping
to make note of some little March thing,
a crow, a chrysanthemum, a deer in a knot of bramble.

The Ravens of Mendocino

How long have they been here? A hundred years or a thousand?
Steadier than onions in the ground. One sign says,
My raven George for mayor. The earth as rotisserie
has already been sold but not yet paid for, but for them,
it's just another good-enough day beside a growling sea.
Last time here, fifty years ago, I said, what do I have to do
to never leave. In the big salt tumble, a deuce of gray whales
work their passage north. Magnolias and cherries
are within my reach. The ravens are the same:
smart, fearless, faithful to a fault. I watch one pair
amble up from Portuguese beach, proud of their status.
Although a flock of ravens is called an *unkindness,*
there's no evidence of such behavior on Albion Street.
Maybe, it's the fab ganja or the antioxidant-rich granola,
maybe it's the community garden and those whales
spouting off the headland that give them a chill omphalos
in an age of unrevealed secrets. I don't want to suggest
they are worthy to hold office but they do make me feel
like the gods are alive and everywhere. Everywhere I look,
another black beauty, fat as a chicken. With a beak as sharp
as the tongue of Moses. Indifferent to the lash of rain
and the thrown crumb. Another sign, *Die by a thousand cuts,*
or live by a thousand greetings. To leap between
the carmine flowering currant and the recent scar of fire,
I will need to summon a throat rattle and a two-footed hop.

Afternoon in the Meadow

The day starts in a coffee shop parking lot listening to a man
picking a fight with his phone for leading him astray.
There are obscenities, body parts mentioned.
It's an ugly, protracted, charmless bickering.
Then, this: the cartwheeling of a blue and white umbrella
the length of Sedgefield Street that made me think
the day was not going to settle down
and I better make peace with the unraveling in the air.
But where in March, named after Mars,
the Roman god of war, would this settling come from?
Not from my sister who has become a recluse
who no longer answers her phone,
not from my lovely Canadian cousin, who asked me
to be her primary eulogist,
not from a fire truck that just clanged down Broad Street
and a garbage can that spilled its evidence.
No wonder I forgot that I found the meadow again,
the flowering cherry and Chinese redbud,
the pink camellia and star magnolia.
Elders with canes and mothers with strollers
and lovers on the grass with laughter
and children rolling and tumbling without supervision.
March, the beginning of the season of war
and this other bursting out from nothing into something
that draws everyone to the meadow
with no need to say how they got there or how long they would stay.

Gold

I climbed to the crest of the trail and paused there
to catch my breath and pass through a gate
and there you were, deliciously lingering like me
to see if you needed more. I just want to say
I acknowledge all you have done to get this far
and I will not think less of you if you decide not to push on.
I've found this business of being in human form
to be both a delight and a disappointment
sometimes in the same moment, but not now
here with you, who must have climbed
from some other route I'm not familiar with.
We could stay here looking out for a while
at the plains lit with late October gold,
that rare color that always seems like something
hammered by the gods and not made for us.
I could tell you the story of my life and you
could tell me yours, touching on what hurt
and what helped. After that, we could go back down.

Dawn Redwood

We had come to that part of the weekend
when reincarnation was the only door left
no one had entered and then, squinting at late night stars
from a beach, someone said I'd like to come back
as a porpoise, another said a hummingbird, then an owl.
The animal kingdom was well represented
and so, I said, dawn redwood.
This tree is not like the redwoods in California
that make your neck hurt. It is short and sparse
and not especially fetching at the trunk or crown,
but it knows something about endurance.
Its ancestors were here 100 million years ago
and it's still found in a few scattered stands
in the lower slopes of the Montane River in China.
I have never seen such a redwood
but I have liked reading about its toughness
to endure so many changes from one age to another.
Not that much happens with such a tree.
The sun goes away and returns, the rain moves in,
moves out. No matter the season,
a tree like this must not be waiting, brooding or lingering
as much as listening to the wind
and drawing up waters from beneath the noise of the world.
I told everyone if I was a dawn redwood,
I could help out with the unending tsunami of problems
coming to plague our children and grandchildren,
but really I was just thinking I could use the help now,
that night, on that beach, under those stars,
to look out at the next dawn and not for a moment look away.

It's the Mountains I Long for. No, it's the Ocean.

No, it's being at the ocean with you and the mountains beyond.
No, it's the green turtles with bulging tumor collars
snoozing on the beach and the mother humpbacks swerving
away from the loopy, oversexed males. No, it's Lightnin' Hopkins
way up the neck, *Come Go Home with Me.* No, it's the way
you wrap your legs around me like an ocean and pull me in
even though I am older than the bones of a mountain.
Every poem I turn to is really a love poem in disguise,
not the first moment of love but the moment after
the lip slather of mother's milk and before the running away
when the old stories fly out the family hope chest
and suck me down, down, down into the craven fields of shame.
These poems still hunger for an aperture, a cave, more lives,
each one reckless to touch the salt that goes on beating without us
and the stone that never blinks, and to be with you,
naked in my arms with the ocean at our feet
and the mountains standing watch for what time remains.

From My Cafe Window

A mother struggles to get her deluxe stroller
folded and put back into her car.
Something has gone wrong with a latch
and she worries her baby will start crying.
The purple saucer magnolia has just opened its petals
and served up all the splash any morning needs.
Three white octogenarians walk by,
each with a lunging shoebox dog
and a different neon hair color
that feels like maybe it could be a new trend
against invisibility and the inevitable chaos to follow.
A twenty-something in a clingy lavender dress
with no bra or underwear
has now come to the window
and is kissing the glass where her partner
sits on a stool on the other side writing in a notebook,
then she puts down her pen,
and lifts her mouth to meet her lover's mouth.
My therapist says that when the baby is in the room,
no matter what else is happening,
The baby is always right. I ask him what he means
and he says, *you know*. That's how our hour goes.
A clarity is offered that is not clearly understood.
The mother finally succeeds while her baby sleeps on.

In a Sea of Trucks

It doesn't much matter where you are in Nebraska, Indiana,
North Carolina, Iowa, Kansas, Oklahoma, Louisiana, West Virginia,
once you enter the shipping lane of the American interstate,
you will have left the land far behind and set down
in a sea of freightliners hauling everything we require
to get through just one more day of everything.
Out there in the convoy, you can get sandwiched
between petroleum and pigs, Fed-X and concrete mixers,
milk and cheese, toiletries, tropical fish, bass boats,
fresh cut flowers, a tank of egg yolks and Red Bull concentrate.
Once upon a time, I liked being locked to the wheel of Rt 10,
40, 70, 80, 90—all the even numbers headed east or west.
I had a girlfriend in Colorado and I was living in Florida
What could be better? My blue VW bug
was my trusted horse and we could giddy-up
to anywhere with a story that would make somebody laugh
with no memory of feeling lost among the giants.
Now, it hurts to sit too long and when I look ahead of me
and see only semis, one behind the other,
an armada balling hard behind tinted glass, I think,
what the hell am I doing out here?
I don't need to wolf another salt and sugar snack while I pump
another tank of fossil fuel. I don't what to buy another thing
that's been diesel-tracked across country.
I want to stay home with the dog
and never go back to a sea clogged with smoke and noise
and the great American economy, unending.

If We had Been Born in California,

we would never have ever left the apricot-colored poppy sprawl.
We would have made babies long before we could afford a house.
We would have known eighteen ways to finesse an artichoke
over fire. How to make a mission fig tart so luscious it could
make a priest wiggle out of his stole. If we had been born
in California, we would know how to swing dance, hunt
for abalone, read the tread of a mountain lion, spot a condor
nibbling a sea lion. White camellias, redwoods, Monterey cypress,
fat and skinny avocados, oranges from Ojai, they are still
plentiful there and almost all the treasure any two lovers
could ever want for their little stay on earth. Last night
you said in the next life let's pledge to be born into California
instead of Akron and Pittsburgh, but let's turn back the clock
before the fires found it and the atmospheric rivers. Let's meet
this time when we are young instead of the age we now are.
In the spirit of the state, we did a Tarot reading, and I drew
the hanged man who told us, *death is not about failure,*
and you repeated something heard on the radio, how regardless
of the next storm coming, the search for survivors continues.

Living Along the River in America

I've peddled by them in Indianapolis and Durham,
San Diego and Portland, Austin, Detroit and Hartford,
the sagging plastic and scrap wood, festooned shopping cart camps
set down along a pretty spill and not so pretty stretch
of jungle brush, weed tree saplings and snags.
Each time, I say, *oh my,* how can this be?
Nobody owns the fucking water, one gent tells me
holding his phone in one hand and a glazed donut in the other,
lucky-ducky that I am on a rented bike,
thinking who doesn't want to live near a river?
Finches, crows, red-tailed hawks, millionaires
and squatters in need of soup kitchens, dumpsters,
bathrooms, libraries, bus stops, and pedestrians with wallets,
all seek the old watery roads that hold the earth together.
On this day in March, the camellias and magnolias are on parade
and a pair of bumble bees have crawled out
of their nesting ground to tumble and chase.
This guy in canary yellow tennis shoes and I
look out at the road and he offers up the epiphany:
What the hell more do I want? Cops don't patrol
the junk trees near the river. It's easy to hide
and I can get a good night's sleep listening to the water.

Sub Rosa Inspection

It's all I know to do, get up in the dark and plant myself in my room,
sometimes with a candle
to remind me how fragile I am before the flame of the actuary table
and still strong enough
to start over, this planting, a decision to seed again in the clay
of early morning
before the house finds it waking. I would like to claim I always
send out green shoots
from my body and turn my darkness into bounty but on many
mornings I just sit in the dirt
of some ancient unknowing and my candle burns down and the sun
slips through the maple.
Other times, I travel with the mole, threading passageways between
bulb rot, glacial till
and the spidery roots gone hideous with age, and there in that lonely
trudge without stars,
I go far enough down to taste the holy water that will open my heart
for another day.
Look, I can hardly tell you this germination is worthy of my time
or that it
always feeds me. I can hardly recommend this route for how you might
enter the *misterium*
of your days and find water, but I do know my soul requires a daily
sub rosa inspection.
Under pressure of an earth torched and flooded by greed, that absorbs
the stones
of our folly and asks only to hold me one more day, there in the vertical
dirt without
a clear path up, I need more of everything, more rope, more shovel,
more bone on bone,
more baring of the teeth to become a willing servant of the buried seed.

The Long Cricket Night in a Summer of No Rain

Beneath the rattle throb of the unsleeping highway,
I can hear the male crickets
scraping their front wings
in the forge of their chorus
which reminds me the world is still here

and still waiting for the rough to be made smooth.
My neighbor gardener tells me
none of the males live long
but they will brave any cinder
to attract a female and protect her at any cost.

Lizards, frogs, turtles and salamanders
all regard the cricket as a delicacy
and now I read there are farms
all over the known world
dedicated to rearing crickets to help feed the billions.

Very soon I will be able to shop
for cricket protein bars,
cricket pasta and enriched powders,
but tonight, I have no need for a meal,
except the one where I listen to other males

filing down the notes that will win another's heart.
Some nights I sweat through a sadness,
thinking how late we met in this life
and how little time is left to us
in these summers of no rain

when the crickets are louder in the furnace
of their music than the traffic grid,
not a one thinking
to feed the speeding world
but only how to get the girl before the lights go out.

Umbrella

It's not a crime to get old and stare too long behind you.
Not a crime to lie down on the earth
and dare her to ease the hours of your distress.
Not a crime to talk with a friend who once
lived in Big Sur until the fires flushed him out
and made him reckless with his grief.
Now, in a room across from a gas station
in Buffalo, he dreams of sea lions and calla lilies.
He's glad for the dreaming, but would rather
be back there with his wife naked in a field
and unconcerned for their nakedness.
So much is still unknown about our hunger
for earthly delights and what it means to spend time
in human form. Naked or clothed, it's not a crime
to sit at God's table and spit out the bitter,
now and then. Not a crime to wish for more
or something less of what we found here?
Like what? To rise by seed or underground stem
and become a soldier that won't quit on beauty
with the still cold Pacific growling beneath.
Like that condor lumbering from a cliff cave.
Before it becomes a god of the long-distance sky,
how clumsy and slow it is like a torn umbrella.

Surfer at the End of the World

I met this aging surfer with charm and thinning hair,
who had zigzagged the globe. He told me wherever he lands,
people say the same thing, *This has never happened before.*
The rain. The fire. Roadblocks on every continent.
Alternate routes over mountains. Snarls of traffic, food shortages.
He also talked of the silver lining: the waves, getting bigger.
Storms more frequent, more thrilling. No matter what happens,
he would be ready. A small thing in the midst of a giant.
I thought of my mother then after a La-Z-Boy collapsed on her leg
and she would never walk again. So much darkness biting down.
Or did I have it all wrong in those last weeks of watching her?
Maybe the petite frame of her, the lightness I could almost carry,
was only removed from the world of matter to be returned to the ocean
of light, whence it came, those big waves waiting to carry her out.

Directions in the Northeast Kingdom
to a Stand of Wild Apple Trees

Across the railroad tracks, past the town dump,
turn left on an unnamed, corduroy road,
and go beyond the cemetery where the few headstones
have been beaten down by weather or worse.
When you see the pale blue bucket on the grandfather maple,
take another left and drive through a colonnade
of peeling birch and hickory.
After a mile or so, a meadow opens to your right
with a creek cutting through it to the far side.
You will need to walk on from there
up the side of a coulee
and there between the edge of a pine forest
and the bones of a farmhouse,
you can find this stand of wild apple trees
hidden behind buckthorn and wild grape bushes.
Knobby, twisted, lichen-covered,
these old ones don't seem to count the years
beyond their ancient age. Lucky you.
Just before the weather flames into fallen rust,
you can sit with them in September
and get hushed with some of your own scaly knot skin.
Once when I was there, I put down a quarrel
started thirty years ago and now I can't remember
the terms of that pig iron misunderstanding
with a woman no longer of this world.
As the deer in the Psalms pants after the water brook,
I long for those apples, forever red and small
but not as sour as you might think
given their long, uncultivated remove from this world.

Fed

The deer return to the swollen river at dusk.
You know this moment of nervous expectation.
Head up high. Ears twitching. Heart forward.
What could go wrong? At this hour of exchange,
I have sent out prayer after prayer without
knowing why I was so desperate to drink.
Then with a glance, the deer are gone and I remain.
Alone with stars. With thirst. With God.
With this memory I have been here
all my life with my fear, my joy abiding.
When you live beside a mountain river,
you bed down in the grass with stars
and you rise in the dark to enter the first pink light
with the idea you might catch a trout
or sit beside this river with coffee and wait
for the fox to whistle a tune and cross
the iron bridge with rabbit in mouth.
Either way, you will not go hungry.
Anything can become something else.
The hook in the mouth, another shining in the eye.

Fig & Elephant

What we ask of trees, we ask only of the long dying.
Suffer more and more relentless heat and blight thereof.
Suffer the locust, the biblical flood, the rogue blade slaughter.
Suffer: to carry enormous weight from below without end.
When I was young, any tree with limbs, a beanstalk waiting.
Help me retrieve the enchanted goose, the harp, the bag of gold.
What will the trees be doing today instead of counting money?
They will clap hands, shout for joy, argue, gossip, get along.
In heaven, God's throne faces a tree. Here, this tree will fall.
And the leaves of this tree shall be the healing of the nations.
I once saw an elephant standing on its hind legs in a squall.
There must be impossible sweetness in the lower rooms of the sky.
My kingdom, this kingdom for one good fig almost out of reach.

The Next Poem

That's the one that will flick the devouring beetle off the raspberry leaf.

The one that will listen to the dribbling of the rain on the roof
and make of it a memory of my sister.

You will still be sleeping in the next room.

The house will hold to the last hours of darkness.

I will be drawing down on my first cup of coffee.

No, that poem has been written.

In the next poem, I will find the photograph from my long hunt.

The one where my father is out fishing with his father
who sits in the bow with his head bent over water,
seeing a mountain at a deep angle that will help his son climb it.

My father wears a floppy hat he always favored on boats.
There is no hint of world wars or drinking
or islands he will escape to in search of a second childhood.

I'm sorry, that poem too, has already been located.

In the next one, I will be half-sleeping like I often do,
and picturing how to give shape to a little world
that does not yet exist.

It too will be made of raspberries, sisters, coffee, mountains,
islands and a boy lit with electricity
for what fish might be waiting in the darkness to take a line.

No one ever knows when the nibble will come

and the morning light will enter the ripple's edge.

That's the way it is with the next poem.

Of this world. Not of this world. Waiting for you to wake up.

Poet in the Pink Jacket

It's never too late for the unwritten page to light a room
with the promise of another boat ride
or the loneliness of a lost chance.
Train stations, olive groves, apricot vendors,
I love how they can still summon the future
out of the past. It's never too late for them.
We've come to that rare place in the story
when there's no longer an intersection
between walking around and the world.
The good news then:
There's still time for the poem
that contains the pencil of an island,
the ping of rain on a tin roof,
a bowl of Pomodoro tomatoes left out in the sun,
the threat of war in the distance.
Once in a mountain town in Sicily,
we entered a church known for its poet in the pink jacket.
In a glass case below a slit window,
he still held a pen and a leather notebook.
I sat with his bones showing through his clothes.
I can't tell you where we went after that.

Rose

Long before the throat tumor the size of a grapefruit
and the diagnosis of a Cancer of an Unknown Primary,
long before the cowboy surgeon at Mayo
who wore alligator boots and a red leather vest,
the one I needed my friend to find,
long before that doctor tickled his tonsils
and found the source, long before multiple surgeries
that gave him five more years, Solly said he wanted
to lay down with a woman one more time
before he died but because of his ostomy bag,
the only women who would do that
were ones who also had a bag attached to their belly
and hidden beneath their underwear.
He explained the stoma is the opening
in the skin where the disposable bag attaches
and the body always carries the hint of an odor
as the stool travels through the stoma
and empties into that bag that never leaves you.
He said as much as he wanted this immersion,
as much as he dreamed of it, and could almost taste
the skin of another on his tongue,
he hated himself for not being able to get naked
with another who wore the same unsightly pouch.
Like he was asking me for forgiveness,
he asked, was it alright, if he only stayed
with a memory of a summer night in St. Paul,
too hot to cool down, when he and his then wife
found a moment of unveiling in the kitchen.
He had just come in from the garden after snipping chives
and basil and their gaze softened for the first time
in months. He dropped the clippers in his hand
and with tears sluicing his eyes,
they each entered the other and from that dust up
with a sperm and an egg, he told me he was convinced

their one child was born, the one they named Rose
because as hot as it was, as unrelenting,
they could see from the kitchen floor
a pink rose climbing the long way up out of the blazing day.

Versions of the Past

In an early novel I wrote that remains in a drawer,
my hero was beset by a belief that death
is the only enemy and then he meets a woman
who is much older who claims to have already died
many times and tells him that life is far more
troubling than anything death can offer.
She lives in a world of grand neutrality
about his entanglements and dreams for their future.
Their sex is plentiful and inventive and though
he feels reassured by its frequency, he fears
she is only accommodating his youth and holds
no regard for his feelings or their future.
At the time, I wanted to write a sad story
so she drowns while they are out sailing
and he leaves his little town on a lake and never
returns to his family who report him missing.
Now, when I consider these characters
still in a drawer, I think of them both
with great fondness, how the boy needs his fear
and his hunger to guide him, how the woman
has stopped gathering evidence and seeking advice.
How they both eagerly shed their clothes and find
in each other a way to make of the hours a new home
where all that they carry, they can also put down.

Black Tomatoes

Last night, while trying to sleep on a sloping
sofa bed, I must have become a worm
cut into pieces by a shovel I never saw coming.
I saw again the dinner party where I had taken
the position that America is now beyond reach
of any shovel but when the pistachio pesto linguini
with mussels was about to be served,
did anyone want to hear my list of reasons?
Earlier in the day, walking down off the Mesa Trail,
and looking north into the gold flake of the front range,
I said to another part of the disheveled worm,
What does it mean to look out at a place
you have always loved and know one day soon
it will be looking back at someone else?
And some other time during that long day alone
in the dirt or the dream, I got my answer with a memory
of picking black tomatoes in late October
with my mother, the last of them, the sweetness
in my mouth cut with a note of salt,
how I wanted that flavor to burn a little longer and it did.

Orchestra Facing the Ocean

Some friends walk into the maw of each new catastrophe and say,
all hell is coming darling so let's get you on home and make some gravy.

Some seek death early and merge with it, others light out for islands
and return decades later with tales no one can believe but everyone
re-invents as if each fabulous escape originated with them.

Some friends run silent like submarines and we wonder what we said
to drive them under so many cold rolling oceans unreachable.

Some friends show up with husbands or wives we can't abide
and we pledge to tell them to ditch their partners before they're
devoured, but we say nothing and pop another bottle of Nero d'Avola.

Some friends we turn to every week like aspirin or bourbon because
even inside dank basements of bitter complaint, they spin threads of
ecstatic ascent.

Some are so gorgeously flamboyant, we worry that age will steal their
loft just when we need them to sugar us into the rainbow strata of the
hidden sublime. Some we can't locate except in memories which can't be
confirmed or denied by anyone, so we launch them again like summer
kites over the ocean.

Some friends dance back off the ledge of near greatness and lunge
into a graveyard of sexual distraction as a way to retain a semblance
of power and mystique which we sometimes envy for its decadence.

Some friends possess such an intimate knowledge of grief it feels like
they're living posthumously only to guide us deeper into the thin places
of our own undoing and we bless them for their new life after death.

Some are more essential than bread or peaches and we will see them at
the end or think about them or remember fondly how they amused or
held us.

Some are playfully unknowable, others we know too well. Some were
not meant to last, though we believed in the promise of their endurance
as we hoped to endure for them.

Who are they all, but notes from a distant bell,
the one just there rising out of a stand of red cedars and then climbing
over the lethal sprawl of traffic. When you next meet your friends,
ask them to be patient.

To put their phones away and wait a little longer for the moment
of arrival.

You are still building a barn at the windy edge of a sloping meadow
facing the ocean

where they all can come before dusk, where your orchestra of choice
will be tuning up for the night to welcome their long-waited attendance.

Another Moment

Everyone who lived on that corduroy road thought of her
as belonging to all of us because every day in summer
she made the rounds of back doors and front porches,
running like a flame across the length of dust,
threading the days with nights, the weave of her time here
a signal that maybe we could do this, be unsheltered
and ungathered from the hours that come from all angles.
We each had our names for this blue-black runner
and we called out from where we stood and sometimes
she came to me and sometimes she ran on and then
she was gone one autumn and that's when I remembered
the day she showed up, how I had been fishing
the upper stretches of the Shadow where the big rainbows
hung back in the green pools and here she came
out of the lodgepole and sat beside me, looking like
this first moment was not something new between us
but only another moment with no need for me to say
what it was or where it would lead beyond our greeting.

Greed

I must not have been ready to meet you until I did,
then again, how close we were, always,
just missing each other in the same towns,
once living on the same street within a shout
and now, in the acceleration of these late years,
if God told me I had to go back to find you
in some early assignation, I wouldn't object to the slowness
of looking more keenly at every passing face,
I wouldn't say I need to be going elsewhere
inside the drifting window of my days,
because it would be worth it to increase the odds
of sooner than later hearing your name,
because you are the one I had always imagined
would bring out my greed for more waking hours.

Meanwhile on Planet Earth,

the gray-speckled fieldstone is still just as old as it ever was.
The goldfish population has not been diminished by our traumas.
The skins of the fat-cheeked heirloom tomatoes
are now breaking more easily
but the juice still runs out of our mouths.
I can't tell if the hidden face of things
is finally ready to emerge or if the fear and greed index
will be the only church left open.
Seems like a perilous time to build a house.
To imagine becoming old on a hill listening to owls
and loons and the leaves rattling against the panes.
A future neighbor stopped by the other day and asked
How are you going to get up there?
How is anything going to happen now that
polar bear is zigzagging south to mate with the grizzly
and the bulletproof glass business is booming
among schoolchildren. How will the lilies in the valley
weather what's coming or is already here?
How do we even trust the stairs
in a world hinged from a cartwheel thread among the stars?

Blue Bathrobe

Every morning, the first thing I reach for
is my blue terry cloth robe just like the one she wore.
In the dark, I pour my coffee by the cup,
then sit at the mercy of my desk.
These days of flame and flood I think I should
seek the Psalms my mother turned to
and find some impossible bridge to cross.
No, it's too late to be spared the fowler's snare,
the long days of smoke, the next pestilence.
Too late to hatch an escape plan.
Among the old now but not even close
to my mother's wild high number,
wondering how she weathered all that time alone,
sitting in the dark like it was her own secret room,
glancing up from her shield and buckler
as a lone gull circled the magnolia just outside her window.
I knew she was getting ready. How did she do it?
Slouched in her mother's favorite chair,
she made leaving look as easy as saying
raindrop, river, ocean, where is my blue bathrobe?
Easy? What did I know of her dash away
and whether she had time to grab everything she needed?

The Pause is the Gateway to Everything

Almost everywhere I go, I hear people joking about guns.
How in the days ahead they will need to know how to fire a Glock.
How they dream about finding an island where guns
are not as common as popcorn. Almost everywhere I go,
I hesitate to look too far ahead without looking over my shoulder,
and then, inside this pale horse everywhere, someone
I don't know will give me permission to keep going,
by stopping to tell me how they just saw a giant bass
leap over a low-slung moon, or a tom turkey flash his junk
crossing the highway, how the world has never looked
so beautiful with every red and gold leaf skittering
before a big November wind. This could already be the last day
of an unimaginable tomorrow or it could be the day
when we first met and I turned around on the other side
of the river and saw you walking toward me over the bridge.

Before I Leave,

I would like to give away my Texas land in Cotulla County
that no one in my family has ever seen
since it was bought at auction a century ago,
those two tumbleweed lots where almost nothing
will grow because the water is too salty
but maybe some illegal family
can find a way to coax a root out of the soil.
I would like to sail again to Block Island
where they manufacture fog in the summer
and if your radar quits or your horn,
you will collide with something much bigger than you are.
I would like to stand out on the tall rocky point
overlooking Lake Superior and take note
of a kettle of red-tailed hawks from Canada
migrating to the warmth with no hint
of the high-pitched descending territorial scream they live by.
There must still be time to locate the Wilson's thrush,
swim with the Hawksbill turtles,
get acquainted with an ancient sourdough starter.
And with you my Sicilian tussle and flowering lilac,
I would like more of everything.
Even that waking after midnight
when we heard women sending out keening notes
through the monkeypod trees,
and the goats and chickens unsettled by the weeping.

Good Morning, Valentine

Now and then, I have this wrangle with someone half my age.
That things are so broke in America,
the country needs to be brought to its knees.
If had to boil down the argument to one line
it would go something like this:
Everything here has failed everyone but the rich.
In this last go around with our daughter Kelsey,
I was tempted to say something like
Growing up means there's no one left to blame.
Thankfully, I held back my dynamite.
Truth told, I often feel the same way *they* does,
but I don't let myself linger there.
Why? In the time I have left,
I don't want my last dance with a broom or a gun.
My hearing is shot in my left ear and my lumbar
is not the best for pushing stuff around.
I don't want to pretend everything is hunky-dory
and I don't want to enter a battlefield.
What is an elder to do? Last night,
I had my first climate catastrophe dream.
Kat and I were delivering a sailboat
and we ran aground, not on a reef, but in the mud.
We couldn't go forward and we couldn't go back.
No one could rescue us because no other boat could find us.
We started to argue about the other's
navigational responsibilities. Imagine that.
In the middle of the mud, another mud-slinging.
I woke in the pre-morning dark and told her everything
and she said, *Good morning, Valentine.*
In the warmest winter in Minnesota history,
with not a flake on the ground of February 14th,
she reminded me our delivery boat was still underway.
Yes, the sea of mud might find us tomorrow,
and we would need to help anyone it might swallow

but today we needed to help ourselves to another feast:
A walk through town for a cup of Joe and a blueberry
left on the rail for that pair of cardinals who look lost for the weather.

And Now This

Almost always it helps to set out over the bridge
and look again for the geese
with their perilous roadside families
braving the cruel complacencies of the world.
Almost always to stop for a coffee
and admit I've been writing one long meditation
on brevity with the remote possibility
of expanse at any moment.
How I can be thinking of some old failure to act
and then stop to greet a stray dog
and then keep walking with less concern
for how I am spending what time I have been given.
I might like to tell you of a terrible truth
but I am probably no longer capable
of anything more than a troubled rumination
and the next hello and a wishing I had brought a biscuit.

It's That Time of Life,

when I appreciate watching a million ants
dragging a dead beetle across a patio,
then up a wall, no matter a thousand times
failing to make the power lift,
and starting over again, then squeezing the beast
out a torn screen no bigger than a pinkie nail,
and failing again but not giving up
as if there's still hope
that the great unending flood of human crimes
pouring in from all directions
might one day find release.
It's that time when everyone I know
deserves a second childhood, a second cup,
a second expanse of small, unnamed hours
for watching such heroic feats,
this turning death back into food for all,
if only there was enough time
and the end of things did not blister faster than the paint could dry
and that one sandhill crane did not
walk into the picture just beyond the screen
where the ants are still at their mighty treasure,
looking lost in the early morning
with its forever mate stuck in the nest
waiting for its one pale yellow brownish egg to hatch.

Juniper

When I grow up, I want to be a juniper in league with the riddles
of the oldest of the old, the shape of my gnarl, the shape
of the wind and rain and what the sand left behind in a hurry,
then when marriages fail, friends die too soon, children vanish,
stop talking or turn away for whatever they must do alone,
I will send down another root to converse with glacial stones,
to be fed each day by fire with no need to dream of the rain.
I could use a shot of that. No, I could kill a whole bottle.
To be out on that lip of a swooning chasm, to hold the bitter
splash of a berry in my mouth and know that even after
a thousand years of fidelity to the emptiness unblessed,
you too with fall the long way down and nothing of what
you recognized at the broad rim will remain with you,
but what a plunge, what a ride, what a way to drop a seed again.

Driving My Friend to St. Paul and Back at Night

I.
All of my friends are older than I am,
from six to thirteen years
which may not sound like much,
but given my age,
if those numbers are rungs on a ladder,
they are nearly at the roof.
My oldest friend said I need to find some younger friends
so I'll have someone to drive me around.
I told him I was driving him to the end.
He said, *you don't know that.*

II.
The manatees in Florida are dying off because the water is too cold.
The eagles in British Columbia starving after eating too much lead.
The monk seals in Hawaii are swallowing plastic
and their small numbers, shrinking fast.

I don't want to live much longer in a world
where there's no need to look up into the sky
and then farther down into blue water.

III.
In a few words, what is going on here?

Always there is loneliness, always longing.

You see this most clearly in the faces of children
walking home from school just before summer break.
And, always hope:
that what we love here will remain,
a single glove looking for its match.

I drive my oldest friend to see his daughter in St. Paul,
then I drive him back.
We talk the entire time.

It felt like we gave our souls a little more food for their travels.

Horses Glimpsed from a Train

I'm thinking here about the terms of our forage.

How I've spent most of my days with this belief:
Life is a runaway train and everything I love
will fall before it. Everything and everyone
will be crushed by the speed of wheels.
No matter how many times I try to get off this train,
I get back on it, but what if I've wasted my life
on this one idea and you and I are really
just horses glimpsed from the train,
those beauties standing in the slough of a field
where everything seen and heard can be spoken of
with a yea yea and a neigh, neigh.
What if our days in the rough field were just the eating of everything?

The Last Tuna Fishermen

We stayed in the rooms where the last tuna fishermen lived.
The water in the cove held us afloat like no other.
We tumbled and spooned and found new ways to make a kiss last.
Before this, swimming was not my longing.
You might regard this lodging as perfect for a honeymoon,
or an anniversary and it was all of that,
a secret place just below a swale of agave and palm
where anything between lovers is possible.
This sanctuary of ochre light and Tyrrhenian sea
also comes with history, the great pelagic blue fin
came here by the tens of thousands every year
since the Etruscans and every year
the fishermen cordoned them with nets,
then bludgeoned, gaffed and hauled in the legends
as they fought to leap clear, the sea gone red
with their failing and the fishermen became famous
just as their fathers had become
for bringing back the big fish that fed so many
who lit the fires for the feast and toasted the sale of the tuna
now packed in ice and now there are no more men
who do this and no more fish, only this cove
where the water holds us for so long we can almost believe
with the blood left in our bones
that we can swim out to any depth and keep running from there.

Problem in the Third Act

The scorpion is hiding in the boot of the general.
The box elder bugs no longer worship the sun.
All the bad money has outflanked the good horse.
In the belly of the beast, more beast.
Our hero can't get home from the sea.
Said another way:
there's a problem in the third act.
Which makes this harbor a place where
I bookend the day, for only here can I imagine
some boat that has never left
will find a way to leave its mooring,
and another will return from a voyage
no one ever thought possible.
Here, a seagull that's always guilty when I'm innocent.
Here, a boat named Goose Bump
and another named Plunder.
Here, the light over the water, a gold rum
rolled over the forehead in an iced glass.
And here on the wall beside me,
a blue cat from the fire and stink of the world.
He's grateful for any scrap I have to offer.
I'm grateful for the company as we dice up the odds,
and for those gooseberry-green eyes washed with the ocean's afterlife,
soft, open, shallow enough to swim in,
and running out to the far blue on a golden thread.

Only a Matter of Time Before the Stone Rolls Away

and the rain returns to the land and the wind comes into full possession
of the government and what's left has to gather
itself somewhere else. What I'm trying to say is,
I'm trying at my late age to wander off like Chuang Tzu
through the folly and suffering
without thinking the world should be my department store
where this box is commendable and this one
is uncommendable and this one should be taken to the trash.
Trust me, I am skilled at labeling the good and the bad,
and telling others at my table what is beautiful
and what is beyond repair, but is that how I want to end my days?
I'm just at the beginning of this new drift and roll
and it's possible I'm still confused about my intention
and it's only a matter of time until my plans take another turn
and I find myself not knowing what to do
when the moon sits down with me for breakfast and the day
becomes the night and my spoon wants to be a fork.

Another Night Above the Highway

Too often at night I get up to visit the tree
and afterwards I stand at the window
with the late-night delivery trucks and cars
still hastening the city.
All I can do is wonder what this road means to them
and what it asks of me,
and where we are going
between the white lines with all this freight.
I can hear the flesh and blood
of every wheel, the rush unending
and the trouble they follow or carry,
the dead among them and the nearly born,
faster and faster our coming and going,
regarded now as congestion worthy of news,
our numbers greater than anyone planned
and so, this insomnia fashioned from the squeal of brakes.
Since I was a boy, I've dreamed
of living on a quiet street with a view of the harbor
and the only sound I would carry with me into sleep
would be the wind from the south
returning to strum the halyards against the masts.

Heaven is a Pig at the Fence

If you live next to a pig, many good things will happen.
She will always take your scraps and make short work of them.
This little recycling will help you feel better about not adding
more methane to the landfill, but here's the clincher.
The world is evermore a sullen face and as you get older
it will see you less, but the pig will always take a gander
and talk freely about this and that. Even if you don't bring slop,
she will greet you at the fence without sudden interrogation.
Whether you are standing in morning light or falling shade,
whether you are innocent, guilty, bound to an old shiver
or trapped by too much heat, you will think, I can see turkeys
pecking at the rabbitbrush and goats and this one piebald pig
with no quit in her for who I am, how I got here, my new limp.

Wind Out of the South

I remember my mother reading to me how the grass flourishes in the morning and fades by evening, but I had no idea then that the grass she spoke of was the same one I walked on with the gathering and ungathering of my hours and now here I am with my seventy years inside the flaring up and sinking of everything except the wind out of the south, brisk enough to whip the cottonwoods and bring a breeze through the blinds. Even in July with no rain for months, this wind brings a coolness that makes me feel like tomorrow will be more available for walking along a river caught in the mouth of a distant sea. I will be there early to catch a glimpse of a fox or muskrat and wish them well for as long as the south wind shall hold them to their hunting which has never served anything but a hunger that must be immortal like the sound of a mother reading.

White Nights

How I hated those nights unhinged from the day.
All those lovers out walking the canals
stopping anywhere for more than a kiss.
Nothing in my marriage making me want
to find more tangle with a sun that would not descend.
But that's not even what I wanted to tell you.
You see we were there with our adopted daughter
on an in-country tour she never warmed to
and she could not sleep with the light
snaking through the hotel curtains
and she wanted to leave, right then,
in the penetrating pink of the night's middle.
She thought her birth country a mistake.
Everywhere, monuments to the war dead.
So many millions our guide said,
no one could ever count them all.
She saw Putin on a billboard,
the one where he enters a hot spring in winter
with shirt off. She saw women dressed in lipstick.
Everything confused her. The stiletto heels.
The men huddled around cigarettes and black cars,
grumbling about the fuckable women.
The night that is the never-ending day.
How in every village, chickens and goats in a brawl
and bread lines held by the old ones who seldom smile
and here in St. Petersburg, the northern jewel,
lovers pawing each other, the cafes open all night,
and water everywhere in a sparkle with no hint of the dark days to come.

I Am What Hunger Looks Like in America

Here I am driving on the two-lane Great River Road looking for eagles.
Yellow stubble fields in a gentle roll
until you enter the first breaks of the Mississippi
and you can feel yourself swallowed
by the glacial shovel that pulled back the clay and iron
and left room for the river to run south to the Gulf.
Pretty country, even this time of year
with the frosted tips of the birch on the bluffs
looking like the entrance to another kingdom.
Beauty then with only a few colors
like the landscape silks of the Tang dynasty
with a small human figure leading the viewer through it.
In which case, I need to point out near Winona
the billboard of a white woman's face
with inscription, *I am what hunger looks like in America.*
This woman does not look sad, so much as serious.
She has taken her pain inside and made of it a study
of the many risks and dangers
found in one more day without time to look for eagles.
That's what I see in her eyes at a glance.
The unwavering hardness of a long journey.
The life of stone under sky.
How long it takes for a river to pour through rock and get to the sea.

Milk & Oil

After the mortuary boys zipped my mother into a black bag,
I could no longer sleep in her apartment where I had slept
in the room beside hers for a month, the night nurse with a swab
and a morsel, so I drove to Wrightsville Beach and sat high
off the sand in a lifeguard's chair listening to the surf travel
from that unbroken place where the salt begins. In the dark,
I held on to the Atlantic breaching the land, each slap helping
to count me back to the hour when I first rocked in her arms
and took her milk. All of that time now like a melted ice cream
in the mouth. Before they came with a gurney that squeaked
when they made a hard right for the hallway that led to a truck
left idling in the lot like another ocean, I rubbed her feet with oil
and thanked her for bringing me into this world, and later
in that chair on the beach, waiting for the pink to tear a hole
in the darkness, I found more time to rub that same oil on my face.

Every Living Creature of All Flesh On this Earth

I can't tell you how much I loved our little driving junket
from Colorado and Minnesota to get stuff I had parked in storage
and was afraid to stare down for how it spoke to the inconclusive
backtracking detours I have always been fond of. Then, presto,
two elders in a real U-Haul truck with big side mirrors
like double-hung windows barreling east. Just south of Lafayette,
Siri gets confused and we stop at a gas station for a map
and the young woman behind the counter says, *What is a map?*
We couldn't stop laughing. That's how it goes with us.

The last time we took a trip together was to pry our sister Anne
out of Ohio. Her apartment, a rat nest, squirrel cage, bowling alley.
And her car, a Flintstone mobile. Ridiculously low to the road.
Anne in the back seat wondering where she was, where she was going.
We didn't know until Council Bluffs, at the neon motel there,
how far she had fallen off the ladder. She got up in the night
and wandered out into the lobby in her night shirt and peed
on the floor. You found her there, smiling through a wrong turn,
and walked her back to the room and in the morning we kept going.

I hoped I still had my wooden sculpture of the Virgin Mary
with blue shawl, head angled down and hands extended,
that Chinese box with a hundred little drawers,
those five star bowls from Africa and the Mexican guitar
with mother-of-pearl neck. Truth is I couldn't remember
what I was retrieving, what I had lost, like trying to read
the writing of the wind in the cornfields. ...and our sister there
in the back seat with no clue about anything, a chasm between us
and none at all, not even the width of the pizza slice in her mouth.

In All Seasons,

I am on good terms with this one walnut tree
that lives on a hill with pecans and hickories.
This walnut has two, earth-touching branches
that reach fifty feet from the trunk.
From the days of the first hard buds in March
until the cracked green shells of August,
we spend many hours together
and I hope to do so until one of us dies.
The chances of me going first are almost certain
and I take comfort from that chance.
When something has carried me off,
I go sit inside this ample crease at the base,
close my eyes and think how this tree is a pioneer
and others of its kind are the first to take root again
after a fire or flood. My mother told me
always to travel with walnuts and if I got stuck
in making a life decision, I should eat one.
The meat of a walnut, she said, is like a second brain.
It's wrinkled, exists in two spheres, and is encased in shell.
If I ever thought I had no one to guide me,
I could park myself beside one
or if I came to a joyless place with no trees, no water
and the darkness of everything had followed me there,
I could just put a sliver of walnut in my mouth.

Pomo Canyon & Shell Beach

Indian paintbrush, yarrow, Mariposa lily.
Meant only for you as a memory of a perfect day.
How we hiked up from the ocean on a fire road,
hugged a trail skirting the Russian river.
How we pocketed the hours for ourselves.
Saw no one. Entered three stands of redwoods,
each clustered around a trickle creek, roots entangled.
How each time we closed our eyes and slept for a minute
with our elders. In the Book of Wisdom,
the wicked believe all is chance and they should grab
as much as they can before anyone blinks.
There you have it, my love. We are the wicked.
The rulers of the earth. At the limits of the chain.
Then, because we are the unwise mouth
that lives to gobble and guzzle,
we found the stairs to a tidepool beach without end,
and there, cobalt mussels the size of a hand
clinging to the exposed basalt stones
and starfish, remember those?
The color of marmalade, saffron, vermilion.

The Coming Together of That Which Is Set Apart

This time, a goldfinch sat on the window ledge looking in.

Like it was waiting for a blueberry or a bible reading.

In the long meantime of my trying not to look back,
it would drift between exhaustion and reverie.

Of course, I could be wrong about this finch.

Wrong about this ledge it had come to
and I was only using this yellow bird
to serve my need to imagine a hidden entrance
to another world where the beginning of something
and the end of everything
are part of the same portal of continuum.

Call me a liar. Call me a man in need of meds.

Call me a man in desperate need of an exit strategy.

Here's my version of the simple, undeniable truth:

The finch leaned into the window and I stood
as a huge, clumsy, monstrous thing in a glaze of shadow,
and we looked upon the other
like the survival of the tribe depended upon
our staying there, at the killing wall of glass.

Once,

This poem wasn't always so quiet. Once, it looked out
the window and counted fires in the distance
and the convalescent stragglers in the haze.
Lost in a low, animal growl, once this poem fed
on the acrid tang of confusion, the rot of autumn,
the pop and hiss of gyrating sparks. Once, this poem
could only say the price of entry is doom. Now,
you might think of this poem as a cross between
a pawn shop with a weakness for guitars and guns
in Wilmington, North Carolina and a sprawling pollinator
garden at the end of a river road in Nova Scotia.
Now, once you enter this poem you will find
a little of everything: the lost arguments of Aristotle,
a shark's tooth in morning surf, a fraternity
of whispered vowels plucked by the wind,
the rusted locks of lovers left on a chain link fence.
Now, any catastrophe is subject to expansion
and the new moon leaves a walking cane at the door.
Now, in this poem, the offering might be like
the warning at the airport, *if you see something,
say something* or someone could be rising in the dark
to make breakfast for someone too sick to get out of bed.

Rendezvous

My sister calls and asks, what are your plans?
I tell her we are making an apartment on the lower level.
For a caregiver in exchange for rent.
She says, *Do it now. Don't wait.*
The last we talked, she said this was her idea
but they have hit a snag.
No one there in Colorado on a river has enough game.
I tell her I will do everything to help her
and John stay where they are.
Besides being too damn expensive,
no one wants to go live in one of those places
where our mother spent the last ten years.
Where you dress up for dinner
and walk past a bud vase left out
for the one who has died that day.
No one wants to enter an elevator alone
and return to an apartment where
no one is waiting with a deck of cards.
We both know how hard it is to die in your own home.
You can't do it without a team.
I tell her I will be on her team.
She says she will be on my mine.
That's where we meet on the phone.
In that wire of last secrets and promises.
Where we are whispering what we can do.
Like we are still children two years apart.
Eager to tell the other what we saw
in the woods behind our house.

Long Ago at Lenin's Tomb

The potato and mushroom and garlic line.
The bread and vodka line.
The line to stand in to get papers stamped
to bring home a daughter from an orphanage.

The line that stretches from a poet's unmarked grave in Vladivostok
to the women outside Leningrad prison
waiting in winter for news of their husbands, fathers and sons.

Sometimes I think I must have imagined
standing in one that snaked into Red Square one April or was it May?

This would have been decades before cell phones
and the lost world of the small screen
craning the neck downward.
I remember soldiers notched into shadows
and a church-like hush to the queue
and how the children gripped their mother's arms.

Putin and I would have been the same age.

Russia had not yet invaded Afghanistan.
It seemed as if this was a time when war was not
the only ragged coat that could be worn.

The day flecked with snow and gray enough to paint with.
Hundreds of people spent hours with me
waiting to glimpse a corpse.
Then, with no explanation, the glass sarcophagus closed.

I never saw the man in a modest black suit on a bed of red silk.
How it is said that his mustache is kept neatly trimmed
and his skin throbs with a gold wash.
Yet all is never lost from all that waiting.

I looked out from my broken place in line,
saw two girls in Basil Square,
how they had peeled away their winter jackets
with light snow falling in their hair
and challenged each other to keep a Hula Hoop alive.

Mandelstam got it right: the smell of oranges lasts forever.

Alone in a Rowboat

I have this copy of a photo of my mother alone
in a rowboat. She is wearing a red sweater
and her boat is red. Her head is bowed.
Her oars rest on the stern. On the back
of this photo she wrote, *Shall I or Shan't I?*
She was one of my best friends and so private
I never knew a single secret she held close.
She started and closed every day with a reading.
I would find her in her mother's chair
with a book open on her lap and her feet up.
When she would weather some new decade
with her sights on the century mark,
and no one left she had ever known except her children,
I would tell her she was so strong and she would say,
You have no idea. For you shall walk out
over the abyss and be held by hidden things,
you shall tremble your fist and open your hand
by morning, you shall die many deaths before you die
and not understand how you found yourself
alone in a rowboat with your head bent.
She told me everything comes down a question
and then I found this photo among her things.
When she died, it was just the two of us in a room.

As My Daughter Goes to Work in a Jail as a Nurse,

I consider all the things that can go wrong.
Most people who enter are not that happy
with their lives and are quick to sell you
on the true story of how they landed there.
Once, I helped teach a poetry class in a prison.
I thought about staying on full time
but for all the rooms without windows.
At the Hennepin County Workhouse,
our weekly class gathered in a basement
like the bowels of ship far out at sea,
with a low ceiling, thin rusted pipes,
recessed lights in metal cages
and a persistent low growl like the rotation
of a propellor. I'm telling you this because
I'm afraid of the mutiny in such places
and I need windows as much as bread.
I'm good with the ocean and I know something
about how to live with the swag of currents,
but many vessels are unseaworthy, right?
I try to tell her this, about such men and their oceans
and she tells me how much she likes
her job and last night she pings a video to my phone.
She is receiving an award for saving a man
overdosed on a drug smuggled inside another's ass.
She is all smiles with plaque in hand,
and then the applause from the big-swelling brine of the jail.

The Soul Swims Out to the Wreck to Have a Look

Not that long ago, this ship was still among us.
Lashed by wind and waves.
The pumps couldn't keep up.
Maybe a second anchor was thrown down
in a last attempt to save the crew.
Beautiful in its disaster,
the way the hope of the last breath
may still sign the articles of another day.
Once you've come out this far,
you can see how the stricken vessel
is a second home for everything.
You can peer into one of many blown hatches
and see angel fish, seahorses,
jellyfish of the transparent moon
and what luck, a red octopus
tucked under a cornice of bearded metal
and one lobster waving spiny antennae
far back in the failed engine room.

In the Chapbook of My Life,

Here, the lake cut with whitecaps
and the tender turned upside down.
Here, my question,
What else is possible today?
Here, my confusion, my wearing out,
the kite I flew over the river,
and the good bike that broke a chain.
After a few pages, it no longer matters
what you remember, what you forget.
There's no one left alive
who can confirm or deny
the glass darkly of whatever story you required.
Here is where you lived for a time
and wrote a few poems
about here and there and what
happened after you told yourself
you were willing to risk everything
in the service of a tree
or was it a boat or a child?
I wish I could say for certain
what held me with rapture at the rail.

Nasturtium Morning in San Francisco

The canary yellow fire hydrant has never faced
so much salmon sprawl and pink orange gold
mahogany, imagine any color you want,

then find it here on this hillside between
the eucalyptus and Monterey Cypress.
Your beautiful life could be winding down

or just beginning at the Dolphin Club, 1877
where, to belong, you must enter the bay
and head out to Alcatraz without a wetsuit,

fins, paddles, nothing but your bright bathing cap
and your own inner nasturtium fire.
That is the takeaway, isn't it, for our times?

To throw off a rambling bloom that won't quit
no matter the heat or cold, to thrive in poor soil.
I am here, you might say to the morning.

Toss me into a salad. Chop me into butter.
Make of me a yogurt sauce or eat nothing more.
I am gorgeously available and abundant at last.

If I Could Think Like a Set of Lost Keys,

I might know what became of the sailboat my father built
in an Amish cabinet maker's barn in Hartville, Ohio
and try to buy it back with remnants of my IRA.
I would find again the back stairs where I met Solly
and he told me of his travels after his last rites
were read three times and then my own
hidden threads might be better seen.
I might travel to the far edge of a parallel dimension
to release my old fault lines
after I told everyone I was free of them.
Truth is, I'm tired of shuttling
between a piece of dirt and a beautiful myth
and pretending I know what to make
of so many unbenevolent unknowns.
Today, tonight, tomorrow, I wouldn't mind
climbing out of a vest pocket and vanishing
where no one can find me and everyone on the search
asks how such a thing could happen.
Where are we always going?
To the long-awaited birth or the next death?
Only the lost keys might show the way.

Leaves, Stones, Shells, Teeth

What helped you while you were here?

From the ends of the earth
and just down a trail from the cove,
only those things sheared from a basalt face,
exhumed by ice, spit from a mouth,
fallen from a crown, left by a ditch fire,
torn from a branch of coral,
only those ragged, long-traveled things
that held beauty and breaking in a glance,
only those things with serrated edge, blush and speckle,
only those things hiding in plain sight
to be nested in a shoe or a pocket
then left for someone else,
only those things worth nothing and everything
and found once only, only those things.

The Bicycle

I heard the recurrent throb and smack of the ocean
and was pleased to be so close to where my ashes
would come to flutter. Gratitude aside, it was much
harder than I imagined to become, unwanted.
Like a ship at anchor, I had grown accustomed
to the sound of my name chafing the throat
of a stranger, the child next door, and my wife
calling out in her sleep, *hey honey, you still there?*
On the other hand, I was sick of corridors with unopened doors,
the unfinished dreams, the geometry of what might
be called last disappointments and accumulations.
I remember little of who attacked and who defended
the old causes I believed in and who resorted
to entering my new situation with a cackle.
My de fault monologue had become a loopy whisper.
I wanted to be here and I wanted elsewhere.
Afterall, this moment had been years in the making
and it was my turn to enter the palpitating hour.
Someone peeled away my nightclothes and socks,
then I took a breath of the many random simplicities.
I pressed my hot face against the cool flank of stone
and in that brief meeting between my skin
and the skin of the earth, I was no longer afraid
to blend my sorrows with the sorrows of the world.

That's when the sea stopped and I heard again the bicycle.

In the Dark Night of the World

What helps me now is sitting with the dying
in the night's bare-assed middle.
Always, they have their eyes closed
and I have this sense, not of their defeat,
but how they are being fed from within
in some way I can't yet imagine.
I used to squirm in my chair or fidget,
read Graham Green or Virginia Woolf
or scan old photos on my phone
and send them to mutual friends.
Now, I too sit with my eyes closed.
I don't bother with the forsaken or the found.
The pretty remembrance or the souvenir.
How I imagine things should go at the end
and who will be there or how long
all this dying time will take.
I just wait out the hours
at the mouth of a blind alley.
This is where I need to be.
Where almost nothing is possible.
My hands and feet touching every limit.

With Some Measure of Remaining Days Uncounted,

this poem resides not on this page,
but in a dystopian future that is still a ways off.
Where from some corner, the mangrove will walk again,
and the seagulls will return to the valley floor
to devour the army of Mormon crickets.

Where if there are any outliers, (what we might still call ancestors),
they will sit again inside a flicker of greenery
and watch the first minnows appear in the shallows.

In terms of how this poem will live now with this future
(That from here feels like a betrayal),
I regret to say that has not yet been sorted out.

Until then, this poem may choose to revisit shock and denial,
anger and acceptance or it may offer only a promise
to remember the sound of things pulling away.

All this poem can offer now is what the frigate bird knows.

Everything can slip off the scrim of the horizon line

and something new can always find the long way back.

The Walk is On

Just above the red bougainvillea leaning out of a stone wall,
you'll find the mud road where four billy goats
like to make it known who is boss.
You'll need to made peace with their horns.
After them, the island road turns even more steep
and your lungs will remind you
how dangerous it is to divide heaven from earth
with any stray thought about anything.
This is another way of saying
you will soon be walking in the clouds
far from the contest and empire that has failed you.
From way up, you will see the long way down
to a calabash tree in the guinea grass,
part flowering limb you are, part goat,
part cloud, part road, part of every clash and quiet
since the first bright rain fell
into a great hollow and became an ocean, the walk is on.

The Hour of Inconvenience

How inconvenient it is now to have a dear friend.
Which in the old Saxon means something more like fiend
or foe. Which also means someone who offers truth.
How inconvenient to drive all that way into the city
for someone who makes me cringe laugh in the same breath.
Once there, in the snarled hub, to crawl through streets
and gaze into the faces of homeless with their scribbled signs
and fake bouquets for sale. To take time at so many stoplights,
then get caught behind a stalled bus and an elderly gent
who has fallen off his bicycle and can't get up. On the radio,
a trio of pundits review the current suffering and the wrongs,
the accumulated hatreds and the new apocalyptic challenges
while I must take one detour then another until Siri
leads me to a lesser street where a child in a Santa suit lingers
the median. How inconvenient it all is to have a friend
who lives beside the Mississippi when I might have stayed back
at the harbor and waited again for the fox who prefers
flirtation to food. She will sit on the stone wall and watch me
hold a cup or read a book then trot off while looking back
as if to say our brief time together is always time well spent.

Palo Verde Beetle

You can almost get it right just by walking out along a river
or talking with a pig or leaning against a walnut tree
with long lichen-speckled arms hugging the ground.
You can almost get it right by staring up into a loblolly pine
to consider a red-tailed hawk with a squirrel breakfast,
then watching it bolt with the remains as the crows arrive.
You can almost get it right by climbing a steep road of goats
who make fun of your need to pause at every switchback
until you reach the upper view of the harbor and the islands beyond.
My best days are within reach of this green envelope
where it's easier to slip inside and say Yes to whatever happens
with a terrible swiftness or an impossible slowness.
Back in my room, I send out email to judges and thugs.
I get worried. I get mad. I finger the links of my chains
and weigh the odds of an ankle turning or a tooth breaking off.
I argue the earth would be better off without the human hammer.
Outside, I can almost get it right. I can tell you about
the wind's velocity, whether the clouds mean business,
and at my feet, I can offer a lusty story about the Palo Verde beetle.
Once the monsoon starts, this armored giant
emerges from its hole in the desert looking for love,
and you can't believe all the trouble he gets into.

The Endless Falling

This poem was started so long ago, and has now traveled
to so many places, I'm come to think of it as a pilgrim
who never left home or a dream stuck on a spiral staircase
that looks down and up through the decades and forgets
whether the above or the below was its final destination,
a poem that set out to help me read the struggles of the world
and instead drifted west to find a café that serves breakfast
before first light. Silly me to enter such a poem that has
never found a way to finish what it needs to say and instead
just circles back through late night escapes and explosions,
stunned by the hours of our "endless falling without falling,"
and remains charmed by the not-so-fat-anymore bumblebees
that plunder the Russian sage, and repulsed by the manifold
stations of radical disparity, and now here I am with January again,
lost and found inside this poem that looks back like a Janus
at the ruins of a journey and is afraid of the future it pretends to see.

Can We Still Speak of Petals in Her Hair?

High cheekbones, wide forehead, a faint slant
to her hazel eyes, a smile that
still loves to hide, my daughter
now a woman with a man she aims to love.
I would like to tell you I can name her ancestors
but they are unknown to anyone.
Horsemen, river traders, bandits, millet farmers?
From the taiga or the steppe?
From the pocket of the Caspian Sea or Siberia?
No matter the inquiry,
no one in Russia can tell her an origin story.
And so, I have this brief one:
Born in Nizhny-Novgorod,
she spends her first eleven months at an orphanage.
She weighs 15 pounds.
She keeps her hands held out as fists.
With a blue ribbon knotted in her hair, she boards a plane.
Nizhny is known for its apple trees.
So many trees that when blossoms come out
it is said to snow again in spring.
The city strung along the Volga and Oka rivers,
the one where Vera was born,
is lit on every street with children running with petals in their hair.

The Authority of Dandelions

Spring is a long way off. I needed to come back.
Where I was, no one knew of my friend.
The acceleration of a slowing down.
How the skin was not springing back.
It's a good thing to say goodbye.
A good thing to sit with others and sing a hymn,
your voice getting smaller
as though you are a child again in the car
before the time of seatbelts
and you have no idea where the road starts.
I still play that game of seeing something
before it vanishes from the window,
the green river, for example,
notched into the mountain's lip,
a woman walking the highway
with her dress torn off her shoulder.
I must be here for a reason, right?
To see something and do something about it.
I can remember sitting in the car with my sister
now gone and we would hold our breath
past the graveyard and not see
something yellow among the headstones,
something our mother saw
and held back with her secret eye.
Those dandelions roaring, *look at me, look at me.*

Variations on the Night

I have nothing against the night except it is too damn long, and you are not in it. The old knots under the facia now talk among themselves with less articulation. The day is far gone; the night is at hand, and there is no suiting up into armor. I saw again my three sisters waiting for me to soldier on from a three-day fever. Walking by moonlight through Escalante Canyon knowing eternity had found us. How many late recriminations will I take to the sandman who must have enough? Nightcrawler, nightingale, nightgown, who isn't facing a habitat problem? Once I could sleep standing up, now the perfect pillow and bed, no guarantee. I peek from the curtain to find honey and rust against a swag of purple pumice. Go to sleep, little one. Nothing can hurt you. Pull up the covers. Say your prayer. Watchman, watchman, what kindness do you bring for the fleeting and unfinished? Out on the ocean in a small boat. Each star like Isiah's burning coal in the mouth. Even when you are beside me, I feel lost and found in these speeding last years. Night is coming. Night is here.

Regarding Those Lovers Who Meet Late in Life

Let us call them two lions circling a kill.
What lies dead between them is everything.
What happens next? There will be a feasting
on the sorrows, the detours, the mistakes.
Others will watch with wonder and horror.
After the pain of legends that have failed them,
they will ask with the shine of battle
for a casual lick, a brush of fur, some old
nourishing held back from the kill.
Happily and slowly, they will drink of this.
Imagine, from such an encounter,
order will return to the entire kingdom.

Little by Little,

I am learning how to walk around without listening
to my own threads about what's not working out,
what's missing, what else has gone wrong in the world.
It's taken so long to get here to this little by little
when I can look out at a marsh and pick out a new bird
in the cattails or see another shade of ochre
beneath the late pecan trees. Little by little,
I am almost falling in love with everything I see.
Just the other day I did not curse the murder of crows
pestering a redtail through the upper sphere
of a failing cottonwood and I held my tongue
when Felix, the neighborhood cat, plucked
another returning rose finch out of the linden.
To witness a life and a death in the same breath.
What more did I require from a morning walk?
Little by little, I am the old one who stops and says,
look up, look down, look there, look now.
Something without a name is calling me
away from my conversation and offering a way out.
Time and it's tra-la-la, isn't it something?

Let's Talk About the Day

I found a faint scribble in the margin
of the novel you were reading,
I am a green olive tree in the house of God.
I wanted to ask you where that sentence
would fit into the morning. Between
the second cup of coffee and the uneaten orange,
I needed to know that after you went out shopping
for bread and cheese, you would return
and there would be time to review
the red-tailed hawk in the tulip poplar.
Just that, a running conversation in a series of rooms
called marriage. The absence of a clock.
Not knowing more every day and wanting
to hear about it. Yes, there will be blight
and nothing will go according to plan, and today
a question about where to find the green olive tree.
Did you see it standing alone beside the road
a thousand years ago or did you only find it while sleeping?

Lucky Dog

Is there any limit to what can be asked of us?

The day could begin with a sparrow
expecting another blueberry on the railing,
and it could end with a brother who calls to say
my name is not Endless, it's Two Months.
Whether you're ready to enter the secret gate to your soul,
or have no regard for such matters,
you could be devoured
or you could be fed by some invisible messenger
and never know what happened
to all that time you had at your disposal.

Which is why when the first pink kerfs of the morning
ask me to go for a walk, I make
a short path to the door,
thinking today must be Saturday,
there's so much left to do, so many places to go,
you, o lucky dog, get to play again out on the river road.

The Remedy for Everything

In my little circle, people talk about leaving America.
Every day, the fear and the promise.
And here I am on a summer evening,
six days after solstice,
walking my former therapist's neighborhood,
headed back to my car parked outside
Eat My Words used books
where you can find the *Five Letters of Fernando Cortes*
and the *Sex Lives of our Beloved Tyrants*.
Until that moment of discovery in the stacks,
in the awning shade, not far from the Tiger Rose Tattoo,
two women in halter tops in a ten-second kiss,
a man in green neon tennis shoes walking his shoebox dog,
a skateboard maven on a skinny, phone bud cruise.
One of those evenings without sirens,
when I can almost forget
that America has once again
gone up on two wheels
and given me this other moment and the sun in my eyes.

In the Next Life, Let's Meet Again Over Coffee...

I haven't said enough about those places that saved me in the morning, just down the street, perched over a bright bend in the river with a view of the mountains, or tucked beside the Gypsy Tattoo and the Last Cupcake, those coffeehouses that brought me friends who knew how to listen, how to argue, tell a joke about a priest and a coyote, offer a teaspoon of victim compassion, recite a line from Chekhov and Szymborska, comment with eloquence and sadness on the difficulties of the world that will only alter course at a glacial pace or not at all, after we are dead. I haven't said enough so I am saying it now because here I am again, among the professional satellite workers, the over-dressed and unbuttoned, old men dozing in corners, those lost inside their phones and those waiting to pick up their order and rush off, the sparrows flitting the door for muffin crumbs and me waiting for my friend to arrive so we can begin again to drift in a dozen directions like a row boat set out on a lake of phosphorus weeds with storm clouds coming on...

At the Changing of the Light,

you are most likely to come across a fox in search of a snack,
pausing on the bridge to imagine
which way provides escape, which way more piglet.
At this moment, the black-eyed Susan
will decide to stand up after the August calefaction
and live to see another September,
and one deer will lead the way to water
by lifting its chest, then stepping forward on low knees.
At this time, the crows will mob the upper branches
of the cottonwood where a red-tail
has nailed a perch over a thatch of voles
and the brown trout will climb out of their pools
to grow fat on the Yellow Sally Stonefly.
This is what I remember of my years along rivers.
At the changing of the light,
the animals are willing to meet you full on.
Like them, you will not know
if you will live to see another day.
Almost everything will give up a shiver
as the light gives way or gains strength
and there the fox waiting at the bridge between the hours.

Rough Sea

When a robin flapped into my open garage,
it must have thought the sky had fallen low
and straight ahead. Lucky, I suppose,
given the speed of a cat, a bluejay or crow,
the robin did not snap its neck.
I found it there slapping wings
against one back window, then another.
I told the robin I could help, but it would
not turn to see the opening.
That's how it went between us.
Me, pointing out the escape.
The robin *like a cork on a rough sea*
as Virginia Woolf described herself
in a perilous room, alone at last.
With each new encouragement,
a greater failure and a weakness gathering.
Then, I shouted *turn around*
and I swear the robin paused its death flutter
and looked back at the world it had fled for all its dangers.

Since Time is the Subject of Every Story,

the catalpa next to the mailbox will fall in a big wind.
The yellow dog at the corner of Division will die barking.
All the lovelies we needed to chase will be forgotten.
The father of the clock will soon pluck our feathers.
The starfield will remember to put us on friend finder.
That said, what's licking chicken, right now, for today?
I was thinking we might want to chat up the purple asters.
I know this trail that switchbacks through shade and sun
and there we can find them in leggy bunches.
Maybe we could lie down in their clustering
and grab a preview of the next galaxy. Over wine,
we often say we wish we had met before sixty.
We would have made babies, traveled on a sailboat
to islands in the stream, but there in the purple,
we could still do it all, meet up and mingle there,
the setting forth calling us out through worry
and wonder like it was the only iffy thing left to do.

However Long You Live,

it's only a few orgasms away from the tenacious wheel of DNA
stuck in the evening of your blood, only yesterday when the wind
caught the smell of lilac and sent you over the bridge to the river
where the fat brown trout leap in the dark of the pink light, only
a thread between fevers when you heard a bell inside the mountain
and you told your three sisters you had to leave them behind
and seek out the distant school of its origin, only a storm away
when the town of your birth was consigned to winter and you
learned how to praise the blade of a shovel, only a gleam ago
when you saw her standing naked beside the tub with a towel
and a ballad in her mouth with no great need to button the day,
only a verse remembered from Isaiah when you first asked God
how to put aside the old things and make ready for a new tremble,
only a curtain blown aside when you glanced at the garden wall
and saw a red-tailed hawk feasting a plump, summer rabbit,
then the rain, then still more, and a slick shine in the morning.

The New Stem

Consider the terms of one La-Z-Boy chair in North Carolina.
Those jagged teeth between the frame and the footrest.
While sleeping, my mother got one leg caught there,
then jolted awake and it happened.
Like a gunshot wound, the doctor said.
37 staples later, she went home, never walked again.
She was already among the oldest of the old.
Already, her skin had turned to paper.
Already, she had begun to lose interest in the fork.
I asked the nurse if I could see the wound.
She told me the body needs protein to heal a wound.
I told her, she wasn't eating.
She cut away the gauze and showed me what she called
The wound that will not heal.
This sounded like an upcoming sermon
posted outside my mother's Presbyterian church
at the corner of 3rd street and Orange.
No matter the mango waffles, coffee ice cream,
fat raspberries drizzled in chocolate,
no spoon of anything was a temptation.
Then, one more dressing of the wound.
When we looked this time, the nurse said,
I can't explain it. What?
Then, I looked down and saw my mother's leg.
Only a month ago, it had been cut back to nothing
and now here it was,
apart from the glow of scissors and blood,
looking like a new irrepressible stem in an open field.

So Many More Stops Along the Bucket List Road,

including the puffin coast of Wales where my ancestors crept
from the moss unlike any other, my father said, painted thick
and interrupted by knots of sheep and the wind raking their coats,
and Capernaum where Christ found his fishermen hauling carp
and catfish and together it is said they hatched the sandal ministry
but first he told them he would only trust those who worked
with their hands and knew something about what fed the world
from the dark nets below, Buenos Aires in a time of the flowering
blue jacaranda which is really periwinkle and I imagine to be
of such brightness it could light the blind steps of Borges after all
his hours at the National Library, the list so long, that viewing deck
in Alaska where the grizzlies grab salmon out of a waterfall
because what animal doesn't know everything tastes better with fat,
the Costa Rican jungle where the red-caped manikin does a high-wire
moonwalk to attract a mate and defies what Darwin claimed were
the only bones for survival, oh let me forget all that glamor geography
and concentrate on a few essentials like the stations of my family,
my neighbors, my sailors who offered a pot of tea to every storm,
what I heard in the trout rivers before dawn, what I hoped and prayed
for my country even as it chose to deny or avoid every blood question,
what I feared when I got sick in the mountains and had to boil water
over an open fire while shitting out everything, maybe just a return
to those fragments and faces that held me, and to one new place,
not yet seen, the most beautiful of all places, where I manage with luck
to remove the last door of hesitation and step through.

Time Capsule Note:
What Was It Like Being in Human Form?

This tightening in the chest,
this holding your hand over your mouth
and sucking back on your teeth.
This merging of your skin with another skin
until the melt of no more questions
took you to the land of I don't care where I am.
This wondering where you are
in the night's train ride to Topolobampo
and the rooster in the luggage rack screaming for sex.
This twitching in your eyelid like a vague diagonal
when the ghost of your father offers you the tiller.
This cramping in your bowels like an ocean
on the other side of the world
because the plumbing has rusted through.
This retrieval of a fishing trip memory that
almost glimmered when you last found it,
then lost it again to the gray plunge of summer days
when you couldn't snag a log.
This recrimination when you remember how easily
you were charmed, then angered,
then repulsed by your own self-assurance.
This unwinding through a bacteria/virus/fungus,
some damn super bug that shot you sideways
through the eye of a needle
and you became the barking dog and the camel,
clutching the hand of nurse Charlie,
this shuttering and unshuttering of your heart
and some very-slow-to-grasp recognition
that the only risk worth taking is the one that hurt you the most,
this writing your name in the sand,
then watching the creeping stain of the tide take it back,
some days you were like the bumble bee

prying open the bent sunflower head even after the sun bled off the page,
other days, this pinching spasm in the back,
this whispering in your throat, what was I doing here...

What We Made While We Made Everything

We made sexy outfits with pockets for billionaire cryopreserved bodies.
We made a plastic island between California and Hawaii
three times the size of France. We made roads in Austin
inside a labyrinth of under and overpasses
to befuddle Siri after the first ask. We made
glass cage condos with elevators starting at $12million.
We made a bottomless landfill outside Las Vegas
that can eat two million tons of waste a day.
We made a computer chip behemoth with 4 trillion transistors
that could run the AI world from one grid.
We made a phone app that shows all the fires in the world at once.
We made a car that can fly over a flood.
We made checkpoints, razor wire, settlements,
with no running water or toilets for the snarled river of feet
escaping from somewhere bad to nowhere better.
Unless you are sitting on a fortune,
we made it almost impossible to die in the mouth of summer
surrounded by animals and the fat of their land.

What Do I Know,

of where the fox now lays its head after the swamp oaks
were butchered and the ravine was backfilled, how to make
sense of the line *on earth as it is in heaven* except to admit
I'm more than relieved my sister Janice will now be able
to push a button when she falls and get a meal brought to her,
who, at my age, could teach me the art of adversarial collaboration
since I still need help sitting in the same room with those
who would paint the street red with their malice, when do I
tell the story of the long-ago stone thrown through a window
that stopped a clock needed to tell a father to wake and feed
a boy before school, what do I know of where to open
the book of dreams that remembers the one where I sailed
alone through raspberry islands and entered another country,
and there, I met a girl who told me I looked like an escapee
from a riot squad, what will I say about this life
at the thin place of my unwinding except I wanted to see
more through the looking glass, it seemed at the time
like the right thing to keep looking for a wing, to stand out
in the rain and wait for the sun to bring up an answer.

Morning Miracle

It's no longer hard to imagine that very slow day
when all the clocks and mirrors merge,
and there is no more trying to get somewhere else.
What's left of the moments will enter us
wherever we are and that ending
could be the last beautiful surprise,
like now, at this beginning of the day,
our bodies scramble, cling, moan, and laugh
and say, *it's a miracle every time*
that we can still remember how to tie a knot
in a bed or better yet, on the floor.
Heat domes, tornadoes, wildfires
all will be coming in greater numbers,
but right now, there's no more waiting,
no more wondering if we need some other morning,
nothing else to say, nowhere to go
but into each other's arms, legs and mouth.

The Still Life in the Room Almost Holds the World

You might think the painting of a bowl of peaches
does not address our apparent lack of a future,
or that it doesn't ask of us a difficult question
about how we intend to give something back
to the morning and that is why you kept talking
about the asshole at the ramp who cut you off.
I get that, and I wanted to tell you I got lost
looking into this painting. Lost, how?
It took me back to a single peach tree I found
on the Maine coast where such trees never live long
because the winters routinely bring ice.
I thought maybe I had succeeded in avoiding
many of the indignities of old age and had
traveled into the next life and been delivered
to this unexpected bounty of creamy pink gold fruit.
But I was still alive, and you were there with me.
More tired than hungry, we lay down under the peach,
fell asleep and when we awoke, we thought
to pick one or two for our troubles.

Heart

There's nothing like the loon we call Larry
doing his somersault laugh over the marsh
to make you think you too can ring the bell
and make a go of another day, nothing like seeing
tiger daylilies standing up after a scorch,
and picturing your bones walking the iron bridge
to meet a friend at the harbor, nothing
like the smell of cinnamon toast to make you
linger the table and tell your truth
about the smoke that entered the window
of your dream and everything else vanished.
Halfway to heaven or stuck in a bardo?
I can hardly offer a description of these days.
I can tell you that Minnesota feels like Florida,
where almost every night the rain breaks loose
and the tree frogs can drown out thunder.
Did you see the heart I left on the front door glass?
I wrote our names inside the condensation.

About the Author

Over the last 50 years, J.P. White has published in well over a hundred journals including *The Nation*, *The New Republic*, *Willow Springs*, *Catamaran*, *The Gettysburg Review*, *Agni Review*, and *Poetry*. He is the author of two novels, *Every Boat Turns South* and *The Last Tale of Norah Bow*. His sixth book of poems, *A Tree Becomes a Room*, was the 2022 winner of the White Pine Poetry Prize. He is the editor-at-large for *Plant-Human Quarterly*.

Acknowledgements

Many of the poems in this collection first appeared in the following publications:

Atlanta Review, Banyan Review, Bodega, Catamaran, Cloudbank, Connecticut River Review, Front Range, Kestrel, The Literary Bohemian, Midwest Review, Pensive, Post Road, Prairie Schooner, Sequestrum, Swing, and *Willow Springs.*

Thanks to Jim Moore for the front cover quote.

Special thanks to my cornerstone readers: Neil Shepard, Jay Hornbacher, Sally King, JM, and Kat White. Without them, this book would not have rounded the corner.

www.ingramcontent.com/pod-product-compliance
Lightning Source LLC
Chambersburg PA
CBHW060333130626
46553CB00003B/1003